EDUCATIONAL ACCOUNTABILITY
THROUGH EVALUATION

EDUCATIONAL ACCOUNTABILITY THROUGH EVALUATION

E. Wayne Roberson

Editor

•

Educational Technology Publications,
Englewood Cliffs, New Jersey 07632

First Printing: April, 1971
Second Printing: December, 1972

CONTENTS

EDUCATIONAL ACCOUNTABILITY
THROUGH EVALUATION

INTRODUCTION

E. Wayne Roberson

President Nixon began the 1970's with an emphasis and a demand for accountability in our educational system. Webster defines "accountability" as "capable of being responsible or answerable." This request appears simple until applied to the complexity of education and its effectiveness.

Actually, President Nixon's request could be fulfilled, if educators at all levels would:

1. Describe their input into the system.
2. Quantify the system output.
3. Relate cost to the process.

"The ambivalence between faith in education and resistance to its costs is present nationwide."[1] It appears that education in our society has become too important to be left

3

solely to the educators. More and more the public and industry are posing questions such as:

1. How effective are the schools?
2. What do we have to tackle today in order to prepare for tomorrow?
3. What relevancy exists in our educational systems?

In order to review what is being done to provide answers to these questions, the Accountability Through Evaluation Institute, held in Tucson, Arizona, April 19-23, 1970, was organized; and the following solutions, examined at the Institute, are presented to the readers of this volume for consideration.

How effective are the schools?

Evaluation of educational programs has become a basic concern to educators. A general presentation of such an evaluation is given by Lee E. Wickline, in the second chapter of this volume. Robinson,[2] Miller,[3] Stufflebeam,[4] Stake[5] and a host of others have devised specific schemes for evaluating change and effectiveness in education. For the purpose of this book, however, the EPIC Scheme for Evaluation has been selected and appears in the chapter entitled "A Scheme for Evaluation" by Armstrong *et al.,* EPIC staff members.

What do we have to tackle today, in order to prepare for tomorrow?

One of the most popular tasks that is being undertaken

by educators today is the conducting of *needs assessments.* There are many theoretical approaches to this task—some of which have been successful and some, unsuccessful. The most common approach is the questionnaire. Generally, opinions and responses are solicited from a selected number of educators, and then categorized in some type of priority format. The results of this type of survey usually yield the "ten imperative needs of youth."

Many times, the current publications and periodicals determine for educators their needs. With the mass media as a vehicle, this has become a powerful tool for determining educational needs on a nationwide basis. In many instances, however, the educational authorities determine their needs on an arbitrary basis. This, of course, is not a valid technique, but it does facilitate the needs assessment by saving a lot of work.

For the purpose of illustration, the EPIC Systematic Approach to Needs Assessment has been selected and is presented by Terry Cornell, EPIC staff member, in the fourth chapter of this volume.

The fifth chapter, by Arthur O. Bachelor, discusses the utilization of Planning-Programming-Budgeting Systems in allocating resources to meet educational needs.

What relevancy exists in our educational systems?

One attempt to add relevancy to what our educational systems are doing is the concept of *performance contracting.* In an effort to expose the readers to the best sources available, two components are examined: (1) Albert V. Mayrhofer of USOE describes the concept of performance contracting (Chapter 6), and (2) the developing role of the educational auditor in the ESEA Title VII and Title VIII programs is discussed by Robert Kraner in the concluding chapter, entitled "Educational Program Audit."

This book is organized to provide the reader with the edited presentations of the Accountability Through Education Institute, and in doing so, to provide insight into some problems and solutions regarding educational accountability.

References

1. Drucker, Peter F. *The Age of Discontinuity.* New York: Harper and Row, 1968.
2. Robinson, F.G. (Ed.) *Emerging Strategies and Structures for Educational Change.* Toronto, Canada: The Ontario Institute for Studies on Education, 1966.
3. Miller, Richard I. (Ed.) *Perspectives on Educational Change.* New York: Appleton-Century-Crofts, 1966.
4. Stufflebeam, Daniel L. Toward a Science of Educational Evaluation. *Educational Technology,* July 1968, *8* (14), pp. 5-12.
5. Stake, Robert E. The Countenance of Educational Evaluation. *Teachers' College Record,* April 1, 1967, *68,* pp. 523-540.

E. Wayne Roberson is assistant professor of education at the University of Arizona and coordinator of field services, EPIC Evaluation Center, Tucson, Arizona.

EDUCATIONAL ACCOUNTABILITY

Lee E. Wickline

Quite vivid in this writer's memory is an exchange that took place between the late Senator Robert F. Kennedy and Harold Howe, who was then commissioner of education, back in 1966. It went something like this. Senator Kennedy asked Commissioner Howe, "What have you accomplished with the billion dollars that you got for elementary and secondary education last year?" In reply, Commissioner Howe began listing the number of books that had been purchased, the amount of money that had been expended for teachers, the amount of money that had been used for the purchase of equipment and materials, and so on. When finished, Senator Kennedy was quite impatient, and asked, "What happened to the children? Do you mean that you spent a billion dollars and you don't know whether they can read or not?" Commissioner Howe countered by saying,

7

"You know this program has been operating for less than a year and it is just like planting a tree; you don't plant it one day and then pull it up every week and look at the roots to see if it's growing." Needless to say, Senator Kennedy was not very happy with this answer.

It was the first brush the writer ever had with demands for educational accountability. That was in 1966, but if one sat in on Congressional hearings today, he would find that, in justifying the expenditures in education, people still talk primarily about how the money has been spent, what kind of materials and equipment have been purchased, the number of children who have been served and the number of teachers who have been involved. They talk very little about what has been *accomplished*.

Demands for educational accountability have been growing. These demands can be traced back to World War II, or sometime soon thereafter, when people became concerned about the fact that a large percentage of the draftees were being rejected because they were functionally illiterate. People started wondering then whether or not schools were performing or were really providing the kind of output that was desired. Later, in the early 60's, there were discussions on the possibility of establishing a national education index, similar to the price index, which would tell something about the quality of education in the United States. Out of these discussions the national assessment program evolved; this program, which just really began in 1968 and 1969, promises to give some idea of the status of the nation's schools and some bench marks as to whether or not progress is being made as time passes. In 1965, when the Elementary and

Secondary Education Act was passed, Congress attempted to build in some requirements for educational accountability. For example, Title I of the Elementary and Secondary Education Act required that effective procedures, including appropriate objective measurements of educational achievements, would be used to evaluate the Title I Program at least annually.

Since that time, and particularly within the last two or three years, it has been found that the parents of children who live in the central cities, particularly minority group members, are demanding more educational accountability. These parents are asking: Why can't my child read? Why can't he get a job? Even more recently, taxpayers in general have revolted. Over the last ten or 15 years, taxpayers have seen federal expenditures for education quadruple. At the state level, expenditures have tripled; and at the local level, they have doubled. People are now seriously questioning whether the increased costs have resulted in equivalent increases in educational benefits.

When educators are questioned about these educational benefits, they are still inclined to talk about the number of books that have been purchased and the number of children that have been involved in the program. They talk very little about student performance. How much it costs to keep a student in school for a year is known, but it is not known how much it costs to increase his reading level one year. Obviously, for instance, a three-grade-level gain in reading in one year at a cost of $1,400 per pupil is a better investment than three fourths of a grade level gain at a per pupil expenditure of $700. Educators are not accustomed to reporting expenditures in this way. However, this situation is changing. Words like "audit," "performance contracting" and "accountability" have crept into the educational literature recently, and they have taken on special meanings in their application to education. The concepts behind these new definitions are appealing to the general public, to parents and to politicians.

One model for educational accountability was introduced by the Bureau of Elementary and Secondary Education and the Division of Plans and Supplementary Centers to implement educational accountability in the Dropout Prevention and Bilingual Education programs. Some of the experiences and problems encountered by these two programs with the introduction of the concepts involved in accountability warrant discussion. First, it should be noted that Leon Lessinger, who was then associate commissioner for elementary and secondary education, developed the concept of educational accountability and was responsible for bringing this concept to the Office of Education. Dr. Lessinger asked the Division of Plans and Supplementary Centers to develop the concept further and to apply it to the two discretionary programs—the Dropout Prevention Program and the Bilingual Education Program—that were operating under the Bureau.

At the time the decision was made to introduce this concept into these two programs, preliminary proposals had already been received and had been funded. To introduce accountability, a small development grant was made available to each of the successful applicants. The grants ranged from $5,000 to $20,000, depending upon the size and scope of the proposed project. Each grant was to be used by its local educational agency to develop a formal proposal, and these agencies were encouraged to use the money to obtain needed outside technical assistance to fulfill the Division's requirements in the following areas: The local education agencies whose preliminary proposals were selected for development were asked to translate their general goals into specific behavioral objectives. They were then asked to compile baseline data on their projects which would tell them where their students were in terms of projected goals, as defined by the behavioral objectives.

They were subsequently asked to analyze and redesign their proposed treatments in order to move the students from where they were to where they could and should be. Of equal importance was the request that the agencies develop an evaluation design which would monitor the progress of the project and provide feedback information to the project director at regularly scheduled intervals to inform him of the progress being made toward achieving project objectives. Such feedback would enable him to modify the project operation and to implement alternative means for achieving the objectives, if he found that the project was not making the progress that had been envisioned. In requesting a more comprehensive, ongoing evaluation system, the Division was asking the local educational agencies to develop an evaluation design which would evaluate the project in terms of the student growth specified in the performance objectives.

The development of this type of ongoing evaluation system was a very important step because, up to that point, evaluation was considered a kind of necessary evil consisting of a pretest and a posttest.

Also included in the requests to the local educational agencies was that they contract with some third party outside of the school district, not associated with the project, to perform an independent educational audit of the project. The educational auditor, who would be a disinterested person, was to examine the evaluation design, monitor the evaluation activities and analyze the evaluation reports. If everything were in order and he could attest to the validity of the evaluation, he would certify its accuracy to the local school district and the U.S. Office of Education. If deficiencies were identified, the auditor would report them directly to the project director, which would enable the project director to make modifications in project operation. This third-party review by the educational auditor would add objectivity and credibility to the evaluation claims of project directors, as well as provide feedback information to the project director which would enable him to modify the project in the first year of operation. Without this type of information, a project might continue for as long as five years with major deficiencies remaining uncorrected, a situation which had occurred often in previous programs.

Much opposition was encountered to the introduction of these concepts and procedures. Project personnel felt threatened. They felt that requirements were being imposed upon them that had not been imposed upon other people who received grants from the U.S. Office of Education. Moreover, some people held a very strong emotional or philosophical opposition to the whole approach of using specific behavioral objectives and being held accountable for specific educational results. Nevertheless, the Division believed that by using this approach, the project would be successful, because its objectives would be well defined and would focus on individual student growth. Project management was expected to improve because of the evaluation system used to provide feedback information to the project director, and his consequent modifications in the project, based upon much more accurate information than he had previously received. Project evaluation was also expected to improve, for more objectivity and credibility could be attributed to evaluation results, since they would have been scrutinized by an independent third party who could either attest to the accuracy of the evaluation or make recommendations for changes in future operations.

Some other problems were encountered as the concepts were implemented. One of the first and most unusual incidents was a case in which the project evaluator resigned as soon as he found out that he was going to have an educational auditor "looking over his shoulder." He said he knew more about evaluation than the auditor did, and if anyone should be scrutinizing anyone, he should be checking the auditor.

Perhaps the greatest problem that auditors encountered during the first year of operation was that of choosing between audit objectivity and project effectiveness. Many of the auditors, when they made preliminary visits to the projects, were quite disappointed to find that many of the projects had poor evaluation designs. For example, instruments were being used which were not appropriate for measuring the objectives the project had developed. The auditors were tempted to begin performing the role of educational consultant to the project, and some came close to doing it. What an auditor should do in such cases is still an unresolved question. Should he advise the project manager of his observations and make recommendations for changes so that the project can be modified immediately, thus increasing its likelihood of success? If he does, he is likely to lose some of his independence and objectivity. The other alternative open to him is to wait until the end of the year when he submits his final report, make the recommendations in his report, and let the project director choose either the outside support group that he would want to use to assist him or from among the alternatives that have been submitted to him.

Another area where problems were encountered is in the area of testing and measurement. Leon Lessinger encountered one of his greatest shocks when he met with a group of testing experts, soon after some of the newspaper publicity appeared concerning the performance contract of the Texarkana Dropout Prevention Project. These experts strongly questioned the use of achievement tests for measuring individual student growth. Further exploration and discussions with testing experts and evaluators have revealed that there are serious doubts concerning the tests. People now are talking about the use of diagnostic tests, criterion referenced tests, and other uses of achievement tests to measure individual gains. Measurement problems were particularly evident in the Bilingual Education Program, since there are very few tests and measuring instruments available that are appropriate for use with children with limited English-speaking ability, and cultural biases are often found in the available instruments and tests.

At the core of the problems and anxieties encountered in the first year's experience with accountability was the fear expressed by many that some of the audit reports might fall into the hands of politicians who might misinterpret them and even use them to the detriment of a program or to the detriment of education. People who felt this way were looking to the report on the Head Start Program that was released in 1969 when the program came under fire; the report was used to recommend that funds for the program be decreased. Their fear was supported and reinforced by the fact that Title I of the Elementary and Secondary Education Act also came under considerable fire during 1969. Since the President's 1970 education message, some evaluation reports have been used either to back the argument that nothing is working in education or to support the possibility that funds used for present programs should be diverted to other areas.

At the same time, from a political point of view, educational accountability has certain advantages. The first positive results developed when the Dropout Prevention Program was discussed at the Appropriations Hearings of the House Committee in 1970. Since there were only ten projects in operation, the project directors were asked to supply better information and more hard data than previously had been supplied. In 1969, the Committee had recommended that no appropriations be made in 1970. However, for the fiscal year 1971, the Committee recommended an $8 million appropriation, which was raised to $10 million by the Senate Appropriations Committee.

Congressional support for education programs is, of

course, crucial, and it is encouraging to see greater support resulting from greater accountability. Even more encouraging are the initial results of the implementation of accountability in the programs. For example, one facet of educational accountability is the use of outside technical assistance. Funds have been made available to school districts, encouraging them to seek such assistance. Consequently, some of the most reputable consulting firms in the country have been involved in a number of the Dropout Prevention projects and, to a lesser extent, in the Bilingual Education projects. The assistance of such firms is resulting in better management, better evaluation and better project management design.

Another facet of accountability, performance contracting, has also had some exciting as well as untoward results, such as the extensive use of performance contracting in the Texarkana Dropout Prevention Project. Unfortunately, this project was not managed and conducted as had been intended. During this school year 1970-71, however, safeguards were instituted to insure that final results would not be contaminated by teaching for tests upon which payment is based for pupil growth. More carefully formulated projects are needed which involve performance contracting, in both the Bilingual Education Program and Dropout Prevention Program. At present, not many school districts want to take the gamble of working with something strikingly different. To this author, performance contracting, when carried out as intended, can provide opportunities for accountability in a measurable, cost-effective way. The Texarkana Project and the concept of performance contracting have received much favorable and unfavorable national publicity. There are critics of both the concept and the project. Some are the same critics who objected to the use of behaviorable objectives. The nature of this criticism can be summarized by quoting from the following item in the November 1969 issue of the Phi Delta Kappan. Although Ed Weir, the author of this statement, may have had his tongue in his cheek when he was saying this, he has verbalized the fears that some people have. Mr. Weir states:

> This old school teacher is just now suffering the most teeth-rattling case of the shakes he has ever experienced. No hang-over either. I have just found out that two school districts in the United States have recently contracted to sell some of their children, potential dropouts, of course, to the highest bidder. The faster students learn reading and mathematics, the greater will be the final payoff. That, says *Education U.S.A.*, is the incentive which moved the Dorsett Educational Systems of Norman, Oklahoma, to make the successful bid. But look at that again. It means that you work the living daylights out of the kids in order to make a profit. And the harder you work them, the more profit you make. Aside from the fact that rapidity in learning is only one factor, and perhaps a minor one in the effectiveness of learning, one might almost describe this development as a new area of education in involuntary servitude. At any rate, it is the manipulation of human beings for private financial gain.

From Mr. Wier's point of view, performance contracting is immoral for two reasons: first, no one should make a profit by helping children learn faster than they have been able to learn previously; second, learning in this type of situation must be an unpleasant experience for the children. But is it more immoral to base payments and permit profits on guaranteed results or to expend funds to pay teachers and to keep children in school, even if they do not learn anything? This writer would also ask Mr. Weir how he accounts for the fact that the dropout rate is much lower in Texarkana's Rapid Learning Center than in the control group in the regular school system. Learning in the Center cannot be as distasteful as Mr. Weir would lead one to believe. In conclusion, these are some of the thoughts and some of the experiences that the Bureau of Elementary and Secondary Education and the Division of Plans and Supplementary Centers have had in attempting to introduce the concept of educational accountability. Without a doubt, the concept of educational accountability is here to stay and will make a major contribution to education in the 1970's.

Lee E. Wickline is assistant director, Division of Plans and Supplementary Centers, U.S. Office of Education.

A SCHEME FOR EVALUATION

Robert Armstrong, Terry D. Cornell,
Robert Kraner and E. Wayne Roberson

This scheme contains four phases: planning, implementation, product and recycling. It is based on Gronlund's[1] definition of evaluation as a systematic procedure for collecting and analyzing reliable and valid information for the purpose of decision making.

Phase I: Planning

Step One. Identify and Describe Variables. The identification of those variables affecting a given educational program is carried out by (1) considering each variable along the institutional, behavioral and instructional dimensions of the Organizational Structure of Variables, and (2) deciding whether or not certain variables directly affect aspects of the educational program which is to undergo evaluation. Once

19

the variables have been identified, they should be described in as much detail as possible in order to avoid misinterpretation. The description of the variables should be clear enough so that anyone could replicate the same evaluation situation.

Step Two. Objectives. The objectives of the given program should be stated in behavioral terms, along with the specifications of how these objectives are to be measured.

Step Three. Evaluation Design. An evaluation design selected should specify (1) the independent and dependent variables of the study, (2) a way in which the variables will be compared, (3) sampling procedures, (4) data collection procedures, (5) methods used to control intervening variables, and (6) statistical techniques which will be used to analyze the collected data.

Step Four. Monitoring System. Included in the Planning Phase should be a description of the monitoring system that is going to be used to check or determine if the planned evaluation procedures are actually implemented.

Step Five. Calendar of Events. The calendar of events describes the sequence of events, dates of data collection and other important responsibilities.

Phase II: Implementation

Phase II begins with the implementation of the evaluation procedure planned in Phase I. During this phase, data and feedback are continually collected using the monitoring system to determine if the implemented activities and procedures are the same as the activities and procedures described in Phase I.

From the feedback collected by the monitoring system,

modifications might be made in the selection of variables, behavioral objectives, evaluation design, monitoring system and calendar of events.

Phase III: Product

The data collected are analyzed in the Product Phase using predetermined statistical techniques. Then, using the results from the statistical analyses, decisions are made as to the level of attainment of those objectives previously stated in the Planning Phase of the evaluation.

Phase IV: Recycling

Phase IV re-initiates the evaluation process by returning to Phase I for the consideration of additional variables and other objectives which might be evaluated in the next cycle. The Recycling Phase implies that evaluation is a never-ending systematic process, and may continue for many years until all variables which are affecting a given educational program have been included in evaluation. In each cycle, a limited number of factors should be investigated in order to maintain realistic control of the evaluation. This control provides opportunity to deduce cause and effect relationships between the factors.

Organizational Structure of Variables

The Organizational Structure of Variables provides educators with a systematic procedure for identifying and describing those variables which influence a given program. Thus the *structure* assists educators to (1) identify variables affecting their programs, and (2) develop behavioral objec-

SCHEME FOR EVALUATION

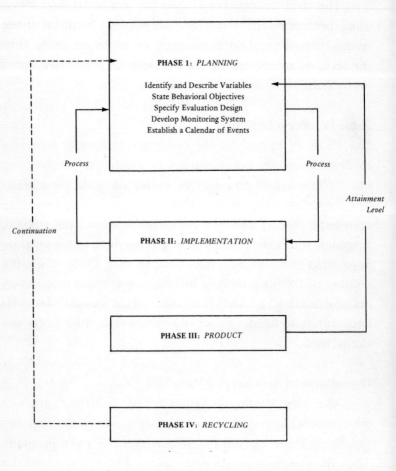

Figure 1

tives in order to evaluate the effectiveness of their programs. In addition, the variables of the structure provide a basis for common communication among educators.

The variables influencing an educational program can be classified in three dimensions. Assuming that education is a process which facilitates behavior change in people, two of the dimensions are *people* and *behaviors*. The third dimension is described in the form of *instructional variables*. These three dimensions can be displayed in the form of a rectangular solid (see Figure 2).

The definitions which follow will help clarify the meaning of the structure.

Institutional Dimension

The *structure* classifies all people along the institutional dimension. The people variables in an educational setting are important considerations. These variables are described as students, teachers, administrators, specialists, families and communities.

Students may be described in a variety of ways. When developing educational programs, it is essential that the characteristics be thoroughly described according to age, sex, achievement level, etc.

The *teacher* variable in an educational program can be described in terms of grade level taught, highest degree held, number of years' experience, etc.

The *administrator* is described as the person usually responsible for the educational program, such as the superintendent, principal or director.

The *specialist* is described as a person who performs a

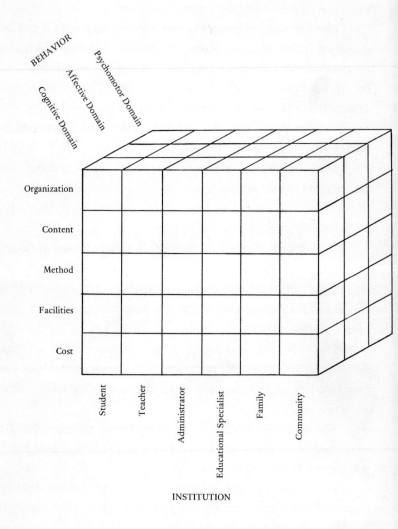

Figure 2

role unique only to a particular instructional setting, for example, a curriculum coordinator, special teacher, etc.

The *family* variable refers to the parents or legal guardian of the child, and includes brothers and sisters.

The *community* variable includes such groups as PTA, service clubs and religious, political and power groups.

Behavioral Dimension

The second dimension classifies variables of people's behavior. The three variables are cognitive, affective, and psychomotor. To describe the variables of *cognitive* and *affective* behavior, definitions from Bloom[2] and Krathwohl[3] will be utilized. The definitions for *psychomotor* variables are those described by Dave.[4]

The six levels of the *cognitive* behavioral variable are:

1. knowledge
2. comprehension
3. application
4. analysis
5. synthesis
6. evaluation

The five levels of the *affective* behavioral variable are:

1. receive
2. respond
3. value
4. organization
5. characterization

The five levels of the *psychomotor* behavioral variable are:

1. imitation
2. manipulation
3. precision
4. articulation
5. naturalization

Instructional Dimension

The third dimension describes the instructional variables or organization, content, method, facilities and cost.

The variable of *organization* refers to the manner in which students are organized for learning, for example, in a self-contained classroom, departmentalized, non-graded, etc.

The *content* variable is defined as a body of knowledge topically described, such as algebra, American problems, reading, etc.

The *method* variable can be described as:

(1) Teaching activities (e.g., lecture, demonstration).
(2) Types of interaction (e.g., teacher-student, student-student).
(3) Learning principles or theories (e.g., operant conditioning).

The *facilities* refer to equipment, space or expendables to support a given educational program, such as reading laboratories, language laboratories, projectors and dittos.

The fifth variable is *costs*. If educational programs are to be completely evaluated, cost in terms of input and output should be considered, for example, how much money was spent in the total educational process.

Developing and Writing Behavioral Objectives
Utilizing the Organizational Structure of Variables

The Organizational Structure of Variables Affecting Educational Programs provides a framework which describes those variables which affect a given program. Variables selected from each dimension interact to form a factor. For example, a *student's cognition* of certain *content* illustrates how three variables interact to form a factor (see Figure 3).

Once a variable from each dimension is identified, an objective can be written. The previously described factor can be used to write a behavioral objective:

At the end of fifth grade, (students) will increase their *knowledge* (cognition) of *reading* (content) as measured by a significant gain on the MOD Reading Test.

Notice that the objective stated includes a variable from each dimension (student, cognitive, content) and describes how the level of behavior will be measured (MOD Reading Test).

In the beginning phases of developing and writing objectives, the following four elements should be included in each objective:

1. The institutional variable
2. The behavioral variable
3. The instructional variable
4. A measurement instrument or technique

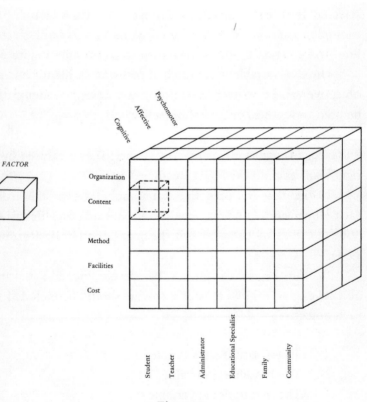

Figure 3

The following questions will be of assistance in writing objectives:

1. *Who* is the person in the institutional dimension of which the behavior is expected?
2. What *behavior* is desired? (Identify the specific level of behavior.)
3. *What* instructional variable will the person's behavior be related to?
4. How will the behavior be specifically *measured*?

The four elements (person, behavior, instruction, measurement) to be considered when writing behavioral objectives are essential. However, two additional elements should be included as soon as the person who is learning to write objectives has mastered the technique. A more complete objective can be written by including (1) the *time* needed to accomplish the objective, and (2) stating the *proficiency level* that is expected.

The following six elements should be considered in order to make the objective more precise and useful for evaluation purposes:

1. Institutional variable (student, teacher, etc.)
2. Instructional variable (content, etc.)
3. Behavioral variable (cognitive, etc.)
4. Measurement (tests or method, etc.)
*5. Time needed (one year, etc.)

* Additional elements.

*6.   Proficiency level (grade equivalent, etc.)

The structure can be broken down into varying levels of specificity in order that one system of writing objectives can be utilized to develop a hierarchy of objectives. Using this format, objectives can be developed for the state, district, school and/or classroom levels.

References

1.   Gronlund, Norman E. *Measurement and Evaluation in Teaching.* New York: The Macmillan Company, 1965.

2.   Bloom, Benjamin S. *et al. Taxonomy of Educational Objectives, Handbook I: Cognitive Domain.* New York: David McKay Co., Inc. 1956.

3.   Krathwohl, David R. *et al. Taxonomy of Educational Objectives, Handbook II: Affective Domain.* New York: David McKay Co., Inc., 1964.

4.   Dave, R.H. National Institute of Education, NIE Bldg., Nehrauli Rd., New Delhi, India.

*   Additional elements.

The authors are with the EPIC Evaluation Center, Tucson, Arizona.

A SYSTEMATIC APPROACH TO NEEDS ASSESSMENT

Terry D. Cornell

One of the most popular tasks that is being undertaken by educators today is the conducting of needs assessments. There are many theoretical approaches to this task—some have been successful and some have been unsuccessful.

The purpose of this paper is to outline the steps that the EPIC Evaluation Center feels are necessary in conducting a valid, informative needs assessment and the subsequent evaluation of those changes which are implemented to eliminate the identified needs.

First of all, a *need* may be defined as the situation which occurs when what is actually happening is below that which is expected. Applying this definition to education, one might say that an *educational need* is the situation which occurs when student performance is below that which is specified in a behavioral objective.

The above definition implies that needs can only be identified through the assessment of stated behavioral objectives to see whether or not they are being attained. *Behavioral objective* is defined as a statement which indicates (1) the behavior that is expected to occur, (2) the situation in which the behavior will be observed, (3) who is going to perform the specified behavior, (4) the expected proficiency level, (5) the time needed to bring about the behavior, and (6) how the behavior is going to be measured.

One might ask the question: "Why is student performance focused upon immediately when considering needs, and not such things as building needs, personnel needs, transportation needs, etc?" Although the latter are very important to consider, it is felt that a much more accurate appraisal of such things as building needs can be carried out if one can determine, first of all, what is expected with regard to student performance, and then see what one must have in terms of resources to bring about this desired student performance. The approach of determining expected or desired student performance first, and then determining what is needed to bring about this performance, attempts to answer the question: "What *should* our students gain from their educational program?" and not the question: "What kind of education *can* we provide our students with our present resources?"

With the above information, one might say: "Okay, I am ready to start my needs assessment. I am going to have all the teachers within the state write the student behavioral objectives they are working toward in their classrooms and then assess them to see if they are being accomplished."

Although this approach has been taken many times, it has some major problems. First, the teacher may not possess the skills necessary for writing behavioral objectives with the previously stated criteria. Second, and probably most important, without any direction or guidelines with respect to the total behavioral change that is hopefully to be attained through a child's educational program within this given state, the teachers more than likely would provide a huge conglomeration of objectives that might be duplicative and/or totally unrelated.

Therefore, a huge amount of time, effort and financial resources might be spent without achieving a network or scheme with regard to what behavioral changes are hopefully going to be demonstrated throughout a student's educational program, when they are to take place, and how they will be brought about. Also, to undertake the assessment of a set of objectives of this magnitude without any notion as to their interrelationships, or without any guidelines as to how they fit into the total educational program of children, would be virtually impossible.

In order to provide teachers at the instructional level with some direction as to the type(s) of student behavioral objectives they should be working toward, some guidelines should be established with regard to how a given teacher's objectives fit into the total plan for a child's education. The establishment of these guidelines simply entails the specification of the steps that will be taken to break down the generally abstract objectives that are written for a total student population into specific measurable behavioral objectives at the classroom level.

For example, if one were to carry out a needs assessment for a total state, the first step would be to write the behavioral objectives at the state level. These objectives would be written for the total student population of the state, and consequently would be quite abstract in nature. Next, the state might be broken down into counties. Behavioral objectives would then be written at the county level for the purpose of defining in somewhat more specific terms what is meant by the state level objectives when applied to each county. In other words, each county may differ with regard to student population in terms of ability, teacher populations and/or educational facilities and, as a result, different behavioral objectives at the county level may occur, depending upon the interpretations placed on the state level objectives. The third step might be the breaking down of each county into school districts. Behavioral objectives would then be written at the district level in an even further refinement of the county level objectives. The resulting district level objectives would fit under the county level objectives, and, of course, the county level objectives would fit under the state level objectives.

This same process for writing behavioral objectives could then be continued to develop the objectives for each school and eventually for each individual classroom. Figure 1 pictorially shows how this structure might look. Given a structure of this type, a teacher is then provided with some directions as to where his students' behavioral objectives fit into their total educational program.

It should be noted at this point that since the state level objectives would generally tend to be quite abstract, they would more than likely be indirectly evaluated through a direct evaluation of the behavioral objectives at the individual classroom and/or school levels.

Given some type of scheme for breaking down abstract behavioral objectives into more specific terms using a series of levels, one must next consider how the objectives should be written. In other words, if a different procedure for writing objectives is used at each level of Figure 1, a problem of semantics may result and communication between the levels would be diminished.

Therefore, in order to facilitate communication between the various levels of specificity, it is suggested that one format be used for writing behavioral objectives. This format would entail the establishment of a given set of variables which would then be defined and used throughout the various specified levels for writing behavioral objectives. The EPIC Evaluation Center has developed such a format for writing behavioral objectives. The variables that are used are displayed in Figure 2.[1]

Instructional Dimension

The Instructional Dimension is that dimension of the model which describes the variables of Organization, Content, Method, Facilities and Cost.

Organization is defined as the matrix in which teachers and pupils are brought together so that instruction can take place. The organizational matrix may be divided into two components known as *time* and *space*.

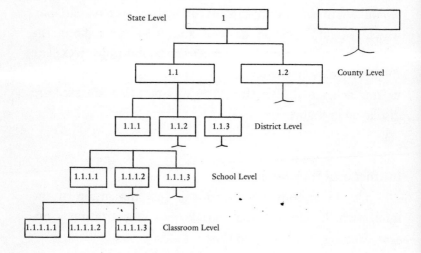

Figure 1

*Structure of Behavioral Objectives
by Levels of Specificity*

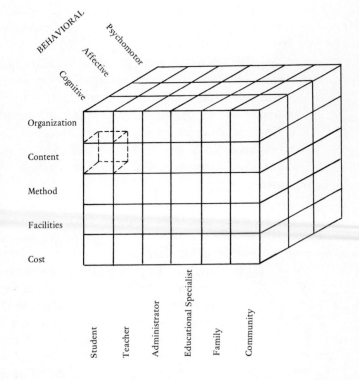

Figure 2

*An Organizational Structure of Variables
Affecting Educational Programs*

1.   *Time* refers to the duration and sequence of blocks of time devoted to the subjects taught. Duration may be defined as the length of any given period. Sequence may be defined as the order in which subjects are taught. Duration and sequence may be thought of in terms of both daily and weekly scheduling. (Example: Science may be taught only twice a week.)

2.   *Space* refers to the vertical and horizontal organization of students. Vertical organization serves to classify students and move them upward from the point of admission to the point of departure. Horizontal organization divides students among teachers. Both grouping processes may be homogeneous, heterogeneous, or a combination of the two.

     a.   *Vertical Organization*: Vertically, schools may be graded or non-graded, or fall somewhere in between.

        (1)   Graded: In pure grading, the content of the instruction program and its sequential arrangement are determined by assignment of subject matter to various grade levels, by designation of instructional materials suitable for particular grade levels, and by promotion of pupils upon satisfactory completion of the work specified for each grade.

        (2)   Non-graded: In pure non-grading, sequence of content is determined by the inherent difficulties of subject matter and the children's demonstrated ability

to cope with it; materials are selected to match the spread of individual differences existing within the instructional gap; and the children will operate according to their readiness to perceive. Promotion or non-promotion does not exist as such. An important goal is to provide continuous progress of each child.

b. *Horizontal Organization*: Horizontally, schools may be organized into any one of many alternative patterns. But all of these horizontal patterns are derived from essentially four different kinds of considerations—considerations of the child, of the curriculum, or of the teacher's qualifications, and of the school's philosophy.

(1) Self-contained: Self-contained classroom is defined as a classroom in which a group of children of similar social maturity, ability, age, etc., are grouped together under the continued guidance of a single teacher.

(2) Departmentalization: The characteristic feature of departmental instruction is that a teacher who is highly trained in a field of knowledge is assigned to teach that academic subject.

(3) Cooperative teaching: Under the general heading of cooperative teaching may be found dozens of different patterns of school and staff organization. Some of these are derived from, or associated with, attempts to achieve greater flexi-

bility in pupil grouping. Others are associated with efforts to eliminate the
administrative and instructional characteristics of rigid, lock-step organizational
structure. One of the most important
forms of cooperative teaching is the
organizational pattern known as team
teaching.

The second variable is that of Content. Content is
defined as that structure or body of knowledge which is
identified with the subject matter of a discipline and controls
its inquiries. Content may be described in terms of specific
topics to be covered at a given grade level.

A third variable is that of Methodology. Methodology is
that process designed to facilitate learning. It may be divided
into three levels: teaching activities, types of interaction, and
learning principles or theories utilized.

1. *Teaching Activities*

a.	Lecture	h.	Homework
b.	Discussion	i.	Review
c.	Question-answer	j.	Individual supervised
d.	Committee		study
e.	Round table	k.	Resource person(s)
f.	Symposium	l.	Field trips
g.	Drill	m.	Inquiry
		n.	Debate

2. *Types of Interaction*
   a. Teacher⟷Student
   b. Student⟷Student
   c. Media⟷Student
   d. Teacher⟷Teacher *

3. *Learning Theory*
   a. Behavior which represents the achievement or partial achievement of an educational objective should be reinforced.

   b. Introduction of cues which arouse motivation toward the achievement of an educational objective will increase the extent to which that objective is achieved.

   c. Practice in applying a principle to the solution of problems will increase the probability of transfer of training to new problems requiring the use of the same principle for their solution.

*Principally team teaching. (In addition to identifying the interaction participants, there are a number of codes that have been developed to describe the interaction, such as: (1) Interaction Analysis—Ned A. Flanders, (2) Teaching Interaction—Marie Hughes, and (3) Classroom Transaction—Stanford University.)

    d.   Since learners differ in their capacity to acquire the desired responses, learning will be most effective if it is planned so that each learner embarks on a program commensurate with his capacity.

    e.   If a pupil has had training in imitation, he is capable of learning by observing demonstrations of skills to be acquired.

    f.   The learner will learn more efficiently if he makes the responses to be learned than if he learns by observing another make the responses or by making some related response.

The fourth and fifth variables are Facilities and Cost. Facilities are defined as that space, special equipment and expendables needed to support an educational program. Cost is the money required for facilities, maintenance and personnel to accomplish a given task.

The variables defined in the above represent important categories to be considered in the educational program. The education program undergoing assessment may contain any one of the variables (e.g., team teaching—organization). Yet all variables must be considered in the assessment of the total program. If the needs assessment is to be conducted on a wide scale, a complete picture of the educational program must be studied with its various components carefully analyzed.

Institutional Dimension

The Institutional Dimension is that dimension of the structure defined by the variables of Student, Teacher, Administrator, Educational Specialist, Family, and Community. Any given educational program will be influenced by the unique qualities of the individuals involved. For the purposes of assessment, each of the variables is described in terms of sub-variables that may have a direct influence on the given program. The following examples are a sample of these descriptive sub-variables:

1. *Student*
   a. Age
   b. Grade level
   c. Mental health
   d. Sex
   e. Familial variables
   f. Socioeconomic variables
   g. Physical health
   h. Achievement
   i. Ability
   j. Interest
   k. Relationship to program

2. *Teacher, Administrator and Educational Specialist*
   a. Identification data
      (1) Age
      (2) Sex
      (3) Race, nationality, religion
      (4) Physical health

        (5)   Personality characteristics

   b.   Educational background and work experience:
        (1)   Undergraduate major and minor
        (2)   Graduate major
        (3)   Highest degree
        (4)   Educational experience
        (5)   Experience outside education

   c.   Environmental factors:
        (1)   Professional salary
        (2)   Professional affiliations
        (3)   Nonprofessional affiliations
        (4)   Socioeconomic status of residence
        (5)   Professional and nonprofessional reading habits
        (6)   Leisure activities outside professional work time

   d.   Degree of involvement in program

3.   *Family*
   a.   Degree of involvement with program:
        (1)   Have children in school; all affected by the program.
        (2)   Have children in school; some affected by, some not affected by the program.
        (3)   Have children in school; none affected by the program.
        (4)   Have no children in school (these are treated under descriptive items in the Community variable).

   b.   General characteristics:
- (1) Ethnic/national/linguistic
- (2) Size
    - (a) Total
    - (b) Siblings
    - (c) Other relatives present
- (3) Age distribution
- (4) Marital status
- (5) Pattern
    - (a) Nuclear
    - (b) Extended
- (6) Income
    - (a) Approximate level
    - (b) Number of wage earners
    - (c) Source
    - (d) Occupation
- (7) Residence
    - (a) Urban
    - (b) Suburban
    - (c) Rural
    - (d) Cost range
- (8) Education
    - (a) Approximate formal level
        - i. Parents
        - ii. Siblings
        - iii. Other relatives present
    - (b) Informal
        - i. Industrial
        - ii. Military
        - iii. Community service
        - iv. Other
- (9) Affiliations
    - (a) Religious
    - (b) Political

        (c)   Social
        (d)   Professional
        (e)   Other
   (10) Mobility
        (a)   Parents' place of origin
        (b)   Length of time in community
        (c)   Frequency of moving
        (d)   Extent of traveling

4.   *Community*
   (a) Geographical setting:
      (1) Location
      (2) Environment—general

   (b) Historical development

   (c) Population characteristics:
      (1) Demographic data
         (a) Population size
         (b) Population density
         (c) Marriage and divorce rates
         (d) Birth and death rates

   (d) Economic characteristics:
      (1) Commercial/industrial organization and development
      (2) Occupational range
      (3) Sources/range of individual incomes
      (4) Sources/range of tax base

   (e) Social characteristics:
      (1) Institutions and organizations
         (a) Government/political
         (b) Educational

      (c) Religious
      (d) Service
      (e) Social
      (f) Commercial/financial
      (g) Labor
      (h) Professional
      (i) Recreational
      (j) Protection
  (2) Power structure
  (3) Socioeconomic stratification

Assessment programs of the past have focused primarily on the child and his response to content in a given subject area. With the changes taking place in educational programs, more evidence is needed as to the influence of the teacher, administrator, parent and community on a given program.

Behavioral Dimension

The Behavioral Dimension is defined by the variables of Cognitive, Affective and Psychomotor Behavior. Cognitive Behavior includes the recall, comprehension and application of knowledge and the utilization of intellectual skills of analysis, synthesis and evaluation.

The second variable in this dimension is Affective Behavior. Affective Behavior is defined as the interest, attitudes, values, appreciations and adjustments of the individual.

Psychomotor Behavior is the third variable in this dimension. It includes those acts which involve neuro-muscular coordination. Handwriting and physical education utilize this variable to draw conclusions about special programs.

Essentially, six questions should be answered when writing a behavioral objective:

1.   What is the Institutional Variable?
2.   What is the Instructional Variable?
3.   What is the Behavioral Variable?
4.   What is the expected Proficiency Level?
5.   What is the time needed to bring about expected behavior?
6.   What method of measurement is to be utilized?

Utilizing this structure, a state level objective might be: *At the end of twelve years of education, a student will demonstrate an increase in cognitive skills in selected content areas equivalent to his grade placement as measured by the state testing program* (see Figure 1, level 1).

One can observe that the

1.   Institutional variable is *Student*.
2.   Instructional variable is *Content*.
3.   Behavioral variable is *Cognitive*.
4.   Proficiency level is *grade equivalent*.
5.   Time needed is *one year*.
6.   Method of measurement is *state testing program*.

Although this state level objective is considered behavioral, it is too abstract to be evaluated directly and therefore should be broken down into more specific terms. Consequently, it becomes necessary for the counties, districts, schools and individual teachers to write behavioral objectives that are more specific with respect to the above six questions.

This task can be carried out by utilizing the structure in Figure 2. The first step in carrying out this task is to identify the factor contained in the state level objective. A factor is simply the combination of one variable of each of the three dimensions. Therefore, the factor contained in the above state level objective is: *Student—Content—Cognitive Behavior* (refer to Figure 2).

The next step is to take this factor and develop a new organizational structure, which should be more specific in nature. For example, at the county level, the factor of *Student—Content—Cognitive Behavior* could be broken down into a number of sub-variables as shown in Figure 3.

The Student variable is now broken down in terms of elementary, intermediate and high school students. The Content variable is broken down according to selected subject matter areas in a given curriculum such as math, science, English, social studies, etc. The Cognitive Behavior variable is broken down according to the levels of Bloom's *Taxonomy.*[2] Consequently, as indicated in Figure 3, the factor of *Student—Content—Cognitive `Behavior* has now become a new organizational structure of variables, but more specific in nature than before, and the resulting objectives using this structure will also be more specific. For example, a county level behavioral objective utilizing this structure might be: *At the end of seven years, elementary students will display an increase in knowledge of English equivalent to the English norms of the Stanford English Sub-Test Elemen-*

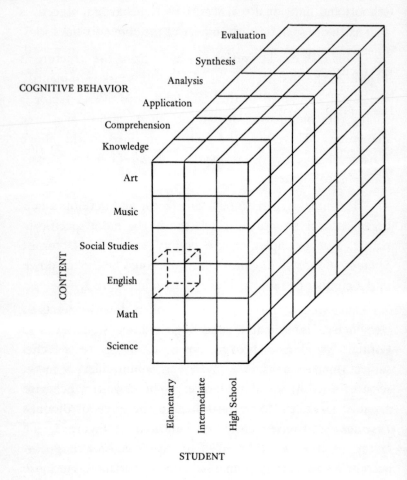

Figure 3

*Breakdown of the Student–Content–Cognitive
Behavior Factor*

tary Battery[3] (see Figure 1, level 1.1).

Notice that this objective (when compared to the first objective) is much more specific. This is due to the increased specificity of the variables which are being used to write the objective, compared to the variables of the original structure. It should also be noted that the evaluation of the new county level objective, which can be classified under the original state level objective, would be an indirect evaluation of the state level objective with respect to level of attainment.

At the district level, the factor of *Elementary Student— English—Knowledge* could be used to develop an even more specific organizational structure of variables as displayed in Figure 4.

The Elementary Student variable has been broken down into Lower Elementary Students which consider grades K-3, and Upper Elementary Students which include grades 4-6. The English variable has been broken down into Reading, Writing, Literature, Oral Expression and Grammar. The Knowledge variable has been broken down into more specific levels of Knowledge of Specifics, Knowledge of Ways and Means of Dealing with Specifics, and Knowledge of Abstractions and Universals in a Field.[4]

A resulting district level behavioral objective might be: *At the end of four years of school, lower elementary students will demonstrate knowledge of specifics in reading equivalent to the norms found on the Stanford Achievement English Test—Primary I Battery* (see Figure 1, level 1.1.1).

Again, one can readily see that the objective is more specific than the two previous objectives because the variables used to write the objectives are more specific.

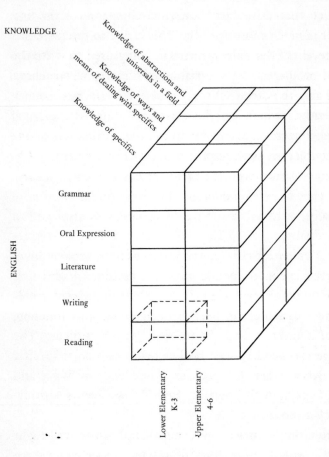

KNOWLEDGE

Knowledge of abstractions and universals in a field

Knowledge of ways and means of dealing with specifics

Knowledge of specifics

Grammar

Oral Expression

ENGLISH

Literature

Writing

Reading

Lower Elementary K-3

Upper Elementary 4-6

ELEMENTARY STUDENT

Figure 4

Breakdown of the Elementary Student—English—
Knowledge Factor

Utilizing the factor contained in the district level behavioral objective of *Lower Elementary Students (K-3)—Reading—Knowledge of Specifics,* a given school might develop the organizational structure of variables displayed in Figure 5. Given the structure, a behavioral objective at the school level might be: *At the end of kindergarten, students will demonstrate a knowledge of terminology with respect to visual and auditory association of vowels at a level necessary to begin reading as measured by the McHugh-McParland Reading Readiness Test* (see Figure 1, level 1.1.1.1).

Finally, to complete the scheme described in Figure 1, the individual teacher would take the factor of *Kindergarten Student—Vowel—Knowledge of Terminology* and develop an even further refined organizational structure of variables. Figure 6 shows an example of a structure that might result.

Using this structure, a teacher might write the following objective: *At the end of the first lesson, Bob will display a knowledge of terminology with regard to the visual and auditory association of the vowel "e" by matching the auditory sound of "e" with a visual form of the letter "e" with 100% accuracy* (see Figure 1, level 1.1.1.1.1).

Again, the variable description has become more specific, and consequently the objective has become more specific. So, in a sense, the same procedure for writing objectives can be utilized to write a very general abstract behavioral objective as well as a very specific behavioral objective. By the *same procedure* is meant the identification of the (1) Instructional Variable, (2) Institutional Variable, (3) Behavioral Variable, (4) Proficiency Level, (5) Time

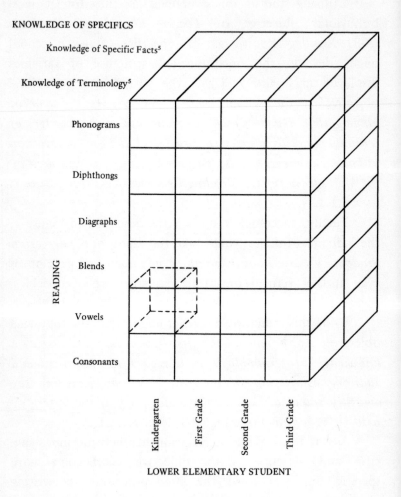

Figure 5

*Breakdown of the Lower Elementary Student (K-3)—
Reading—Knowledge of Specifics Factor*

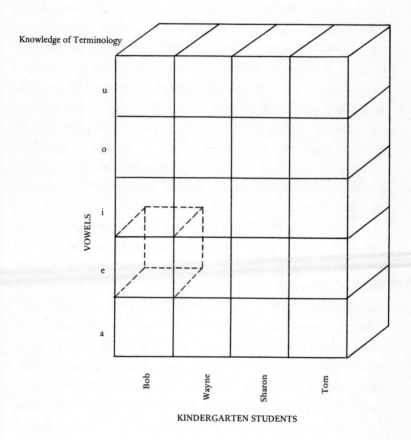

Figure 6

Breakdown of the Kindergarten Student—
Vowel—Knowledge of Terminology Factor

needed to bring about expected behavior and (6) Method of Measurement. The only difference in the objectives is that one is more specific than the other because the variables are more specific. However, no matter at what level of specificity objectives are written, a structure of variables derived from the original structure is utilized. One can readily see that the Organizational Structure of Variables Affecting Educational Programs really has an infinite number of levels of specificity, and the given level of specificity that an educator uses to write the behavioral objectives of an educational program will depend upon the amount of time he intends to spend in accomplishing the objectives. In other words, as the degree of specificity increases, the amount of time needed to accomplish the objective tends to decrease.

Also, as pointed out in Figure 1, by using the same procedure of writing behavioral objectives at various levels of specificity, one is able to trace back through the various levels of abstraction and determine the level of attainment of any objective at any level of specificity. This procedure might eliminate many of the problems that confront educators today with respect to the large gap that exists between state level objectives and how they are operationalized at the instructional level. Consequently, the results might be a more accurate appraisal of the degree of attainment of those objectives which are written for very large populations and more insight into needs assessment.

It should be emphasized that although an example of a state needs assessment has been used to describe how the Organizational Structure of Variables can be used to write behavioral objectives at varying levels, the same approach can be used to conduct a needs assessment of, let us say, an individual county and/or school district. The only difference would be the levels at which behavioral objectives are written.

Once the behavioral objectives have been written at the various levels of specificity, the next step should be to evaluate the objectives, beginning at the instructional or classroom level and continuing through the higher levels, to determine which objectives are and are not being met. *Those objectives which are not being met according to the specified proficiency levels create, according to definition, the needs of an educational program. In other words, what is actually occurring is below what is expected.*

Once these objectives which are not being met are identified, the next step should be to determine what is needed with regard to resources in order to accomplish the objectives and then to compare the needed resources with those presently available. This might be termed an *assessment of the curriculum.* Figure 7 indicates how one might compare the needed resources to the present resources.

Figure 7 is only one example of a curriculum assessment inventory and, of course, could be expanded to many different categories such as organization, methodologies, content, etc. The important aspect of an inventory of this type is that it allows for the utilization of much of the data collected at the state level through survey instruments and relates this information to specific objectives. More than likely, once the inventory has been completed, one will find that the reason most of the objectives from the needs

Objective: Ninety-five percent of the children at the end of the second grade will increase their
                  knowledge of the sound and letter of all single consonants found in reading material of
                  the second grade level to a level where they are able to associate them with 75 percent
                  accuracy as measured by teacher observation and oral and written assignments.

Curriculum Component	Inventory Questions			Now	Needed	Match-Mismatch	Comment
SCHOOL PERSONNEL	*Do we have the personnel to meet the objectives?*						
	Teachers:	Ratio of classroom teachers to pupils by grade					
		Number of teachers with more than three years experience					
	Instructional Specialists:	Number available in					
		Math					
		Reading					
		Foreign Language					
		Other					
	Special Services Personnel:	Psychologist					
		Psychomotrist					
		Counselor					
		Speech Therapist					
		Librarian					
		School Nurse					
		Other					
	Paraprofessionals:	Paid Teacher Aides					
		Volunteer Teacher Aides					
	Food Service Personnel						
FACILITIES	*Is our present school plan adequate to implement the objectives?*						
	Is sufficient classroom space available?						
	Are multi-purpose rooms available for small group and large group instruction?						
	Is the school library of sufficient size and supplied with enough books and materials?						
	Does the school plant lend itself to the mobility of students?						
	Is sufficient storage space provided for housing materials and equipment?						
	Is the playground area large enough to serve the student population?						
	Are teaching stations adequately equipped for the comfort of students throughout the year?						
FINANCES	*Do we have the money to proceed?*						
	If not, are current district funds sufficient to implement objectives?						
	If not, what other sources of financial support are possible?	Federal					
		State					
		Local					
		Private					
	If not, has nature of need for additional funds been identified?						

Figure 7
Curriculum Assessment Guide

assessment are not being accomplished is that what is needed and what is present are totally different. The next step should be to determine if the mismatches can be eliminated. Many mismatches cannot be eliminated because of such things as cost; and, therefore, the decision might have to be made either to eliminate the objective from the total educational program or to rewrite it to be accomplished with the present resources. For those mismatches which can be eliminated, a change is identified which should undergo evaluation to see if it does in fact lead to successful accomplishment of the identified objective(s).

Scheme for Evaluation

The EPIC Evaluation Center has also developed an evaluation scheme which can be used for the purpose of determining whether or not the change in educational resources does lead to the successful accomplishment of the identified objective(s).

Figure 8 displays the EPIC Scheme for Evaluation.

Definition of Evaluation

Evaluation may be defined as a systematic procedure of collecting and analyzing information for the purpose of decision making.

PHASE I: Planning

1. *Identify and describe variables.* The identification of those variables affecting a given educational program is carried out by considering each variable along the behavioral, instructional and institutional

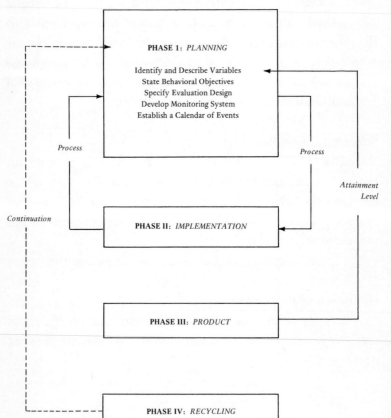

Figure 8
Scheme for Evaluation

dimensions and deciding whether or not it is directly affecting that aspect of the educational program which is to undergo evaluation. Once the variables have been identified, they should be described in enough detail so that one can readily interpret the effect each variable has on the results of the evaluation. In addition, the description of the variables should be sufficiently adequate for one to replicate the same evaluation situation in all respects at some future time.

2. *Objectives.* The objectives of a program should contain the following information:

    a.   Institutional variable
    b.   Instructional variable
    c.   Behavioral variable
    d.   Proficiency level
    e.   Time needed to bring about desired behavior
    f.   Method of measurement

3. *Evaluation design.** An evaluation design is a specification of:

    a.   the independent and dependent variables of the study,
    b.   ways in which the variables will be compared,

* See also the chapter "A Scheme for Evaluation."

    c.   sampling procedures,

    d.   data collection procedures,

    e.   methods used to control intervening variables, and

    f.   statistical techniques which will be used to analyze the collected data.

4.   *Monitoring system.* Included in the planning phase should be a description of the monitoring system that is going to be used to determine if the planned evaluation procedures are actually implemented.

5.   *Calendar of events.* A calendar of events should be drawn up to describe the sequence of events in terms of data collection and other important responsibilities.

PHASE II: Implementation

Phase II begins with the implementation of the evaluation procedure planned in Phase I. During this phase, data are continually collected using the monitoring system to determine if the implemented activities and procedures are the same as those planned in Phase I.

As a consequence of the information collected by the monitoring system, changes might be made in the (1) variables affecting the program, (2) behavioral objectives, (3) evaluation design, (4) monitoring system and/or (5) calendar of events. On the other hand, changes could also be made in Phase II, to implement more effectively what was originally planned in Phase I.

PHASE III: Product

During the Product Phase, the data which are collected in the Implementation Phase are analyzed using the appropriate statistical techniques. Then, using the results from the statistical analyses, decisions are made as to the level of attainment of those objectives previously stated in the Planning Phase of the evaluation.

PHASE IV: Recycling

The Recycling Phase re-initiates the evaluation of a given program back to the Planning Phase for the consideration of new or additional variables, and in turn, new objectives which might be evaluated in the next cycle. The Recycling Phase implies that evaluation is a never-ending process and may continue for many years until all variables which are affecting a given educational program have undergone evaluation. The Recycling Phase also implies that in each cycle a limited number of variables should be focused upon in terms of investigating their effect on a given educational program, so that control of the evaluation situation and procedures can be maintained. This control provides more opportunity to deduce cause and effect relationships between the variables rather than just an overall description of the situation.

Summary

In summary, this chapter has outlined the steps that the EPIC Evaluation Center considers in the conducting of a needs assessment. Following these steps one would apply a systematic procedure for collecting and analyzing reliable information that could eventually be used to make valid decisions with regard to the attainment levels of a given set of objectives. These decisions would eventually assist educators in answering the call for "accountability in education."

References

1.   EPIC Organizational Structure, EPIC Evaluation Center, Tucson, Arizona.

2.   Benjamin S. Bloom *et.al. Taxonomy of Educational Objectives. Handbook I: Cognitive Domain.* New York: David McKay Company, Inc., 1956.

3.   If the Stanford English Sub-Test—Elementary Battery is to be used in assessing a child's increase in knowledge of English, it becomes necessary to distinguish between those test items measuring knowledge and those measuring such behaviors as comprehension, application, analysis and/or synthesis. This would tend to increase the content validity of the measuring instrument. Therefore, since many standardized instruments are used to assess student performance, the EPIC Evaluation Center has developed guidelines which can be used to code test items with regard to what level of behavior they are measuring for a given group of students.

4.   Bloom, *op. cit.*

5.   Bloom, *op. cit.*

Terry D. Cornell is coordinator of the Evaluation Services Division of the EPIC Evaluation Center and assistant professor of education at the University of Arizona.

PLANNING-PROGRAMMING-BUDGETING SYSTEMS

It does not matter what kind of a handle you put on it—we're talking about a management system when we refer to Planning-Programming-Budgeting System. We are talking about a management system that can be incorporated in a school district. It has been tried and proven in industry and in some facets of the government, and we are trying to develop a system that can help us in education.

Limitations of Traditional Budgeting

There are certain limitations with object classification accounting. First of all, and I think primarily most impor- tant, is that in a typical object classification type of budgeting there is a difficulty in relating your budget to your objective. You deal in terms of administration, in terms of instruction, in terms of capital outlay, maintenance—you don't really work in terms of trying to relate a budget to the objectives of the district. Secondly, it is a poor basis for resource allocation. Traditionally, budgets are developed by asking: How much money do we have this year, and how can we spend it? Thirdly, the traditional concept of budgeting has never been a convenient tool or a good means of projecting expenditures into the future. Any time that budgets are projected into the future, traditionally, it is done by adding six per cent for salaries and the cost of living and then trying to pare it down into your available income. Fourthly, there is difficulty relating expenditures to accomplishments. Any time that there has been an effort to relate expenditures to accomplishment it has traditionally been *after* the fact. How much did we spend in this program last year? How much did we spend trying to accomplish this last year? It has been difficult to try to recoup this type of information.

Let us say that we have a foreign language program in the 6th grade in the district. We can collect our costs on it, and we can assess to some degree the productivity of this program, but there are alternative ways of teaching this program. The traditional approach to budget has never really been a tool by which we could assess these alternative ways of trying to accomplish our end goals. Finally, planning, budgeting and control are generally not integrated. Control is a very important aspect of Planning, Programming and Budgeting Systems, because there is a high degree of responsibility and accountability.

Definition of PPBS

Very simply, a PPBS is a systematic approach to the application of limited resources for the attainment of priority objectives. There really isn't anything new in PPBS. We have all talked about goals and objectives. Boards of education have beautiful philosophical statements about what the district is supposed to do. And we have curriculum guides that have established goals and objectives. They may even go into the methodology. And we have budgeting and we have accounting and we have evaluation and we have some system analysis. *PPBS pulls all of these elements together into a systematic system.*

When applied in an educational setting, a PPBS provides decision-makers with the tools to plan and develop programs which will further the instructional process, to evaluate these programs and to provide long range fiscal data so that choices may be wisely made among alternatives in striving for fulfillment of the district goals.

There is nothing magical about a PPBS. What you have is a tremendous increase in the amount of information available for staff, for administration, and for the board of education. They can then use this information in making decisions about the activities of the district—where it is going, how it is moving and what plans are to be taken in the future. Again I would emphasize the fact that there is no magic in a PPBS. It is a very much improved method of developing and providing information for those people who are faced with making the ongoing decisions about the school district.

Elements of PPBS

There are eight elements of a PPBS:

1. Goals
2. Objectives
3. Measurement Criteria and Evaluation
4. Program
5. Program Structure
6. Program Codes
7. Program Budget
8. Multi-year Financial Plan

Goals. A goal is a statement of broad direction. A goal is general and timeless—that is, it is not concerned with a specific achievement within a specified time frame. Keep this in mind. This is a goal as opposed to an objective.

Let us take a look at some examples of some goals. "To develop individuals who in terms of their potentials can appreciate and understand the many forms in which communication occurs (verbal, non-verbal) and who can communicate (read, write, listen, speak, view and act effectively) with understanding." Very broad, very general, timeless, no measurement criteria essentially, no evaluation—a very broad goal towards which a district might be working. "To have fundamental skills and understandings, enabling them to meet and solve problems qualitatively as well as quantitatively." Doesn't say how any of these are going to be done at this point. Or, "to appreciate the value of the sciences and understand the purposes and methods of sciences, observation, experimentation, recording, analysis and prediction."

Or, "can make realistic appraisal of their interests, their aptitudes, their achievements." These are some examples of some very broad, general, timeless goals.

Objectives. Here we get a little more specific, a little more definitive. Objectives are desired accomplishments, which can be measured within a given time frame. Achievement of the objective advances the system towards a corresponding goal. Accordingly, objectives must be developed that support and contribute to the achievement of the established goals. Let us take an example of objectives. "By the end of the 8th grade the student will know, with 90% accuracy, ten lists of 8th grade words selected from the Basal reading test." An objective must contain four elements: who, what, and when, and it must have a measurement criterion attached to it. Also, it must have some means of evaluating the success in reaching that objective. Objectives do not deal with the how or the where, since those are generally reserved for methodology. And they don't deal with why, because why is generally incorporated within the goals statement. Note the more defined specificity of the objective as compared to the goal.

Measurement criteria. This refers to the way in which we are going to assess how well we have met the objectives. Measurement criteria are the means by which the accomplishment of objectives is measured. Measurement processes may be subjective (by observation) or objective (by testing) in nature and must be established concurrently with the objectives. Objectives and measurement criteria are only of value when found together. They are cumulative in nature, are more definitive and detailed at lower levels and provide a framework for planning, action and control.

Program. This is a group or a package of interdependent, closely related services or activities, progressing toward, or contributing to, a common objective or set of allied objectives.

Program structure. A program structure is a hierarchical arrangement of programs which represent the relationship of activities to goals and objectives.

Program codes. Programs are coded to facilitate the collection of data such as cost and statistics in regard to student participation, staff needs, etc.

The program budget. The program budget in a PPBS is a plan that relates proposed expenditures to programs within a specific time frame. It includes the proposed revenue sources for financing those programs. As I indicated above, we have been accustomed to identifying costs or developing budgets in very gross classifications—administration, instruction, transportation, etc. Under a program budget concept, we begin to deal with budget and costs in the same way that industry deals with them. In other words, we talk about salary costs, benefits costs, supplies and material, and capital outlay. These are the elements that industry relates to in their cost accounting. So, under the PPBS, we will be relating to these same elements of costs. In traditional budgeting, we have a big classification called fringe benefits in which we collect all the costs of health and welfare and retirement, under one big classification, with no attempt to distribute that cost back to programs, back to teachers, back to custodians.

Similarly, we distribute inter-program charges. Suppose

our instructional materials department prepares a group of transparencies for the foreign language program. In the past, it has not been traditional to identify that as a cost to the foreign language program. Under PPBS, it is very definitely a cost of the foreign language program.

The multi-year financial plan. A multi-year financial plan distributes or projects costs into the future. In the past we have dealt with progression by percentage. When we start dealing with programs, we can be a little more specific with our needs. For instance, in our physical education program, we are going to be able to project that three years from now we are going to have to replace the trampoline, or in the business education program two years from now we are going to have to replace 50% of the electric typewriters.

In Berkeley, we try to budget our resources across the board so that we do not have rich schools and poor schools. We may have some schools that may need some additional funds for one reason or another. In other words, the principal and the staff are going to have to come in and they are going to say, "Look, our library meets only 25% of the A.L.A. standards and every other school in the district is at least at 50%. So we've got to have some more funds for the library." Why do you have a need for more money, and what are you going to do with it? These, I think, are the kinds of things that a board of education and a superintendent and an administration can respond to more intelligently than just saying, "We're a poor school and we've got to have more dollars."

Accountability

One other element of any management system is the factor of *accountability*. We need to involve staff at all levels of development and this, of course, is where the element of accountability enters the picture. Who becomes responsible for what activities and to what extent are they given the authority to exercise their responsibility? Once we move into the operating arena, be it classroom, office, or elsewhere, those persons with prime responsibility for meeting objectives and goals must be given the opportunity to select their method of operation.

In Berkeley, we have tried to involve school staffs in the development of the school budget, and we have given the school the latitude of selecting its methods of meeting program objectives. There are times when the Board of Education has not been able to meet all of the budget requirements, but our staff has not used this as a cop-out to avoid having to meet the basic objectives. Rather, they have displayed the desire to adjust their methodology so as to try to meet the objectives within the fiscal constraints. Obviously, this means that some objectives may be missed. Accountability doesn't mean that at this point the Board points a finger and cries "shame." In any good management system, this is the time when the responsible parties identify the reasons for failure to meet all the objectives—be it shortage of staff, space, dollars, whatever—and the Board then has sufficient information to make meaningful management decisions.

PPBS won't solve all the problems of education; no management system will. Still, it gives all those persons interested in improving education—board, community, staff, students—a vastly improved system in which to try to interject improvements. A PPBS isn't something that happens overnight, either. It takes time, and it takes commitment and, to be very honest, it should never be completed—because it should be a tool to be used in doing our task a little better; and that can always stand improvement.

The Berkeley Unified School District and the citizens of Berkeley have pioneered many meaningful improvements in the educational field. In 1968 Berkeley became the first large city to fully integrate its school system, and also in 1968 it was a vital participant in the formulation of a state PPBS. We are proud to have had these two opportunities to make meaningful contributions to the improvement of our public education system.

Arthur O. Bachelor is director of business services, Berkeley Unified School District, Berkeley, California.

NEGOTIATING A PERFORMANCE CONTRACT

Albert V. Mayrhofer

It is the purpose of this report to call attention to performance contracting and accountability as applied in Titles VII and VIII of the Elementary and Secondary Education Act. One has to be politically and socially astute when opening up a contract, because he is going to have to live with it, as well as with the news media and educational critics. It is, consequently, good judgment to have a general statement of purpose and justification when initiating a contract. This procedure would not be grossly different from the kinds of things already being put into contract proposals. However, a general statement and justification of purpose would provide a correspondence between the proposal and the contract. It could cover such areas as improving reading or math, and would state that such an approach is educationally and financially sound. A general position could be taken which states that the situation has been studied and that the contractor does, in fact, have something to offer.

Contractor Accountability. The next point which should be recommended is a general statement that the contractor has agreed to be accountable. It should describe the decision that the contractor's service is sound—educationally, politically and socially, in terms of district goals, that is, things that are long established in the district's statements of intent. Next, spin-off benefits should be considered. (One can be flowery about this because this is not the tight, legal part.) In-service training, and how it can benefit the district, should be mentioned, along with sharpening and tightening evaluation. It is an excellent opportunity to reach the general public. They may not be able to read the rest of the contract, and the purposes stated in this first portion serve as general communication. Cost benefit comparisons, between what the district is doing and this particular service, the public can understand. Remember, there are many audiences. Another excellent way to bolster relationships in the community is a statement of the desire to bring the resources of the private sector to bear directly on improving the learning of the community's children. The public does not share, in general, the white hat-black hat game that educators have played for many years. Many of them think educators are pretty foolish. A protective device—a strictly protective device—is a general statement of the source of funding. Set the ball park on "where the money is coming from." It may be a federal source or the funding may be consolidated, that is, maybe federal, state and local funds will be used.

Obligations of the contractor. These should be spelled out. If these obligations are left for later, disagreements may arise, and they can injure the whole intent of the operation. Remember, a contract is an agreement. It is a promise someone makes to deliver goods or services, or a combination thereof, for a consideration. And that cannot happen in a vacuum.

District obligations. District obligations unfulfilled can lead to a fiasco. It is wise always to remember that industry, which has had much more experience in this field, never knowingly promises anything it cannot do—and neither should the district. Because situations arise in which additional needs develop as follow-ons to the obligations of the contractor and obligations of the district, a procedure should be included for how these will be resolved.

Total payment amount and the schedule. At this point, one should start to become precise about the actual dollars and time to be spent. Set precise dates. Lack of specifics can result in much confusion and many hurt feelings and arguments later. Under the *money and time* heading, describe the reduction criteria and amounts. The terms "reduction criteria and amounts" are used rather than "penalties." There are no penalties in contracts. Both *reduction criteria and amounts* and *incentive criteria and amounts* should be handled in a consistent way.

General payment schedule. The next important point is to describe the offset against the general payment schedule, in detail. If one describes his offset formula and then he buries the details in some other part of the contract, a referencing problem is probable. Consider how the offset will be made, at what point, at what period in the schedule. Protect both the contractor and the local education agency (LEA). At this point it is wise to put in any demures that the local district would have. If there will be a grant, a federal grant, then the whole contract should be made subject to the federal grant conditions and amount. Because what was applied for may have been reduced through negotiations, it is important to put in a statement that adequately covers the subject of the actual delivery of money. The fact that a proposal has been negotiated for an amount is no guarantee of receiving funds. Some kind of a national or state crisis could come up. One should also have a statement spelling out that his intent is that the sub-contract will not be, in any case, 100 percent of the grant.

Performance guarantee. Who is going to do what for whom, the target population, the procedures that will be used, the conditions, the time, etc.? How is it going to be measured? When? By whom? What instruments?

Statistics. Are they going to be based on individual improvement or on group improvement? If on group improvement, one had better come to some understanding of whether or not they are going to be based on mean achievement. If they are based on mean achievement, one might want to put in some distribution ranges. There are all kinds of ways. Then, very precise payment terms should be considered. One can use tables or he can use formulas. However, specification of statistics should be clear and in detail. Be sure that everyone understands and that it is fair.

Reporting. Is there an agreement on forms? What are the procedures for filling them out and collecting the data?

What are the dates, not only for the production of the forms or putting them into use, but what are the actual reporting times? This is important. There are many elements that go into an operation. To whom are the reports sent, by whom, and when?

Personnel is a very important item. Who is the project director and what is his authority? Is there a project director for the local education agency? Is there another one for the corporation? Are two used? Iron it out. Find out what kind of an agreement can be made that is practical, but most of all functional. Of course, this has to be linked into the particular school district's operation at some stage because the superintendent of the district is the responsible agent. It is very wise in negotiations of this sort, when one arrives at this stage, not to forget that the superintendent is there. He may have delegated the job to the performance contractor, but there are times and critical points at which the superintendent should be brought in and his judgment sought. He is the man where the "buck" stops.

Teacher cooperation and competence. Maybe the contractor is going to hire teachers from the school district involved. Maybe they turn out to be incompetent; or someone has an automobile accident; there is an injury. Maybe a teacher looked good in pre-service. Suppose then something happens and it turns out that the original judgment was wrong, or something happens to the teacher. In all fairness to the contractor, and mostly to the students, it wouldn't be fair to keep that teacher there. At that point, one has to have procedures previously agreed upon as to how to resolve this problem. It should be suggested that the performance contractor bring the teacher groups in. They have a right to have an input here.

Teacher pre-service and teacher in-service. It is even more unfair, both to the students and to the person who is on the firing line—the teacher—to be thrown into something with no training. Arrangements for pre-service and in-service have to be made if one is going to achieve any short- or long-range benefit.

Teacher constraint on the use of alien material or procedures. No teacher has a right, as far as the students are concerned, or as far as the contractor or the district is concerned, to bastardize a system which has already been contracted. The teachers who are going to do so will usually be volunteers. They are generally the kind of people who will not do it if they understand it is not to be done. No more than an agreement in the contract and a signed understanding with every teacher who participates is necessary. If they, in their judgment, feel that supplementary materials or procedures are necessary, the written permission of the project director should be required. No fancy language is needed for this. The idea is to get communication and clear action—team action.

Calendar and time total. A contractor will not be cooperating in all probability unless these items are included. What about Acts of God? What about teacher strikes? What about fires, lightning and tornadoes? The contractor cannot be held accountable if the children are not there. For the educators, it is not so much of a problem, but performance contractors are getting paid on the basis of what they do. It is very important to state this in the contract for them, and what the constraints will be. Will there be a shift in the tables or in the formulas according to days missed? There are many ways of handling the problem, and they should be considered.

Data. What about the contractor rights to statistical data, both during the program and later, as far as publication rights are concerned? What about identity protection of a school, and, of course, of the children? Invidious comparisons could be made by people who do not have the background to be able to make judgments, and the school and students should be protected. There is something else that should be discussed as a matter of good business practice. If a contractor is also a producer of hardware and software, or the packager in an overall copyright system, he will want to sell items. That is why he is in business, and he will look very kindly toward anything which helps sales. Contractors usually have a high level of confidence, demonstrated by their good guarantees. Educators can usually reduce total costs in the operation during negotiations by giving the contractors the right to publish the statistical data, as long as they maintain the anonymity of the groups and individuals involved. Publicity is worth as much as money to them; it is the best advertising they can get. It is in the enlightened self-interest of public education to be cooperative.

More funding constraints. One can be very precise concerning funding constraints. The precise nature of the funds should be identified as well as the source of the funds and the schedule of the funds. What are the normal and tolerable limits on non-delivery? What about a fund cut-off—

an interim fund cut-off? Everyone has the flu in some state capitol and the federal money coming through the state cannot be delivered on time. Maybe a computer breaks down. These items should be covered. What about listing limits of the district liability in these cases? As far as the contractor is concerned, what is negotiated is not punitive. It is getting an understanding and an agreement. What about the total term and damage liquidation in case the project has to be cut off entirely? A liquidated damages clause is extremely important. It can cover ten, twenty, thirty or sixty days. This is a matter of negotiation and agreement. But it must be stated. All the other conditions should be included. Then there are the items, "successors and assigns," by which parties should be bound. Conceivably the most well capitalized company in the world could suffer and get into very difficult problems. It has happened in the past to corporations in which there were key people at the top who were killed on an airplane. What happens to the companies? They are absorbed by someone else. Consequently, contracts should cover the heirs, the executors, the successors, the assigns and administrators in the school district.

Sub-contracting constraints. This can produce very troublesome situations. If one is going to have constraints, they should be detailed.

Assigns, mortgages, incumbrances and interest transfers. Here one should go back to exclusivity of funding. However, this time it is to protect the district as a legal entity. It should be specified that no bills can be sent to an administrator, and none can be sent to a board member, jointly, individually, by court action or other means.

Performance bonds. What about the possibility of a bond—a performance bond—based on the degree of capitalization of the corporation and its reputation? In talking with legal and financial people, one hears, "What difference does it make? The contract will cover performance and, in the end, the educational system will end up owning the equipment." What about the students if equipment breaks in the middle of a semester? The students have to be protected.

Miscellaneous. A general clause may be inserted which includes the students, their parents, back to school night or anything else.

Data responsibility. What about patent, copyright, and publication rights? Is a story going to be written about the program? Who is going to write it—some teacher, some administrator, some contractor or someone working for the contractor? What about the data? What about a history of the project? Who owns it? What about materials which are developed right within the project? Who is responsible for dissemination to the public? It should be one person, and even this can be sub-contracted for as a service. When one is a project director, working for the company or for the project itself, he could be totally distracted from his work because of the amount of publicity he will have to handle. This problem should be addressed ahead of time. Data dissemination is a service which will have to be rendered and there will be no options on it. One approach is to use some of the system analysis procedures.

Litigation. One important consideration is a clause in which local, state and federal law, where it is applicable, governs the interpretation; litigation should be, by contract, in the home state. If this clause is omitted, the litigation may be brought in another state. Many publishers, for example, get their charters in states that have great advantages to publishers. Those same advantages may not extend to the particular school district involved. A clause should be included covering these matters.

Then, of course, there are some of the "boiler plate" items: the purchase options and conditions—who owns what, and when. Lease options and those kinds of things can be taken up at this point, as well as insurance.

Future price of equipment and materials. What about an escalation clause for inflation? It could conceivably put the project out of business. It is necessary to be fair to the contractor on this point, because his costs may go up. It is possible to arrive at a fair inflation escalation clause, and that is, in the writer's judgment, the amortization life of the last piece of equipment bought in the actual contract. However, this price should be accompanied by a delivery guarantee. It does no good to guarantee a price on a non-produced instrument.

All these agreements are meaningless, unless one inserts a turnkey feature in the contract. If one contracts and receives a performance 100 percent better than that anticipated, according to student learning, and if nothing is done to insure more student progress in the future, nothing has really been done to strengthen the teachers' and administrators' competence, and nothing of a lasting nature has been accomplished.

A turnkey feature must be included, along with a *display* of the numbers of personnel and their costs, the system design and its costs, management and its cost, and logistics and its cost. Maintenance and schedules are the areas that people neglect. Schools are notably, across this country, totally unmanaged. Not mismanaged, but totally unmanaged on these matters; maintenance schedules, parts inventories, machines and their stocking are necessary to keep the down-time to a minimum in the classroom; space, transportation, and data collection procedures are needed to know how to buy wisely, and how much of what kinds of things to purchase. This will help the entire district operation, and the turnkey feature is a good way to get into it—a good entry point.

None of this will happen unless an RFP (request for proposals) is available. The RFP will determine the kinds of contracts and proposal submissions which will be received from the private sector. At this point it should be suggested that most districts need a management support group that understands these matters. Most school people do not have the experience.

It is important to have that management support group in the beginning. If it is missing, there will be nothing but real sorrow. At present there are few, if any, institutions of higher education in the United States which have addressed themselves to some of the major problems in education. Big universities have schools of business and finance, but somehow or other fertilization does not take place. Several local states have done some work, and the federal government has done some work. Colleges and universities are now taking note of these effects and are making changes. However, in the interim, management support assistance—technical assistance—will be needed.

Questions and Answers.

Question: What exactly is the turnkey feature?

Answer: The turnkey feature, ideally, would be a performance guarantee to provide the district with the training and the system and management mechanisms necessary to carry on and expand the operation, should the district choose to do so. The contractor cannot be held responsible for what happens afterwards, because that is a district problem. However, criteria can be set for determining whether, in fact, the training, the data collection procedures, and the organization of all systems and management policies have been done.

Question: How large a contract should be considered when initiating performance contracting?

Answer: That's a good question. Performance contracting should be used on any contract that met or exceeded the bid requirement in each particular state. The contract should be limited by the state accounting manual requirements for bids, as a good rule of thumb.

Question: Does a contractor have any ground rules as to which students are to be involved? Is it a situation governed by a particular school, a particular age group, etc.? How is the student group established?

Answer: It is negotiated in part by who does what with whom under what conditions.

Question: In a school district where there is a severe reading problem, there are children whose reading ranges from one year below the level to 4.5 years below. As the contractor, would I take the one year below and work with them, or do I take them all together?

Answer: That is a district problem; the request for performance stipulates what the district expects. The contractors may come back meeting that goal in terms of their proposals or bids. However, they may also come back with alternatives with different patterns of funding. And that's a matter of negotiation. It's very wise in the RFP to give the private sector as much room as possible on alternatives, because it may have some ideas not previously considered.

Question: Who does the contracting?

Answer: A local educational agency, or a consortium of them, contracts with the private sector to meet a problem that the district has not been able to meet. Performance contracting certainly can apply to work with the federal government. The U.S. Office of Education does performance contracting in many different areas. Performance contracting could be done with EPIC for evaluation or for auditing.

Question: In applying for funds, should one apply for federal funds first?

Answer: It is a good idea, but suppose one has a very large problem and does not know what legislation is going to come. He addresses the problem, receives an RFP, and, suddenly, some new legislation takes place. One shouldn't wait for legislation to address itself to the problem because, as discussed earlier, the idea is to improve the delivery of service to students. Performance contracting is only one aspect of accountability. There are many ways of doing it. The RFP should not be too hard to generate if some technical assistance is provided. There is nothing wrong with submitting the proposal, though.

Question: Offset criteria and incentive and *reduction*

criteria were mentioned earlier. Please elaborate on offset criteria.

Answer: Let it be assumed the contract states that the contractor will be paid $100,000 a year for a particular job. That is the total amount. All right? And payments will be made, $50,000 by the middle of the year and another $50,000 at the end. Maybe it will be split up into $25,000—let's run it that way. Let's say that $25,000 is to be paid in the first quarter, but only three days before the payment is to be made, one discovers that the contractor is going to suffer a reduction. Are there bookkeeping facilities adequate, in three days, to go through and change the whole procedure? No. Therefore, a point at which this is going to be done must be established—next pay period, perhaps. The offsetting occurs, and the $25,000 is paid. There is nothing illegal about the procedure, as long as one makes note of it and it is offset against the next pay period. However, if these details are not worked out, logistic and legal problems might result. Offsets here provide one with lead time.

Question: Suppose a lawyer draws the contract up. What is the cost?

Answer: A lawyer should look the contract over and take care of the heirs and the assigns, the liabilities, and all the "boiler plate" items. However, technical assistance people, who have both education and private sector experience, and management support group people should work with district people in writing the contract. Attorneys, businessmen or anyone else has no right to determine how things should be done. They have to be derived from the RFP. One might even want to use a different kind of technical assistance, such as an honest broker, when the bids come in. Have a third party review at that time. Maybe some of the professional people from local colleges and universities, or perhaps some of the business men and attorneys in the communities would be willing to review these things. There is a sufficient degree of professionalism left in this country that they will do this, in situations where schools are under duress for money and other reasons, at no cost.

Question: Is the only criterion for payment to the private sector student performance?

Answer: No, the turnkey feature might be another criterion for payment, listed as one of the performance guarantees.

Question: If a contractor came in and provided "X" number of hours or man-days of service, could he be paid for that?

Answer: He could, but it would not be wise.

Question: Would the incentive be student performance?

Answer: Certainly, and one can use a fixed fee. Or one can have just straight incentives. There are many ways it can be done, for example, extreme reduction, on one hand, and incentive, on the other. It can be done on a fixed fee basis: The contractor does not get paid anything if he does not make it.

Question: The feature of how performance contracting was written into Titles VII and VIII and possibly into other key areas was discussed. If one is a representative of a school district and wants to write a proposal in a particular area of interest, what would be the first step, the second step, etc.? If one is not familiar with the area of business in which he is interested, should he ask for recommendations from the U.S. Office of Education or from outside sources?

Answer: As a matter of public policy, the U.S. Government cannot go around recommending this group over that group. It would not be fair. But it can answer, as far as its experience goes, on the reliability and competence of people. There is, however, enough information around now, if one just reads newspapers, to find competence. In regard to the question of how to obtain access to this, Titles VII and VIII *did* have management support or technical assistance set aside for school districts for that very purpose. It did not mean that the districts had to go into performance contracting, but they did have to have management support to get an organized project, and there was money for this.

Question: Who specifically should be contacted and what problems should be addressed when initiating a contract?

Answer: First of all, it is impossible to make decisions in the absence of information—not data, but information. One should have a needs assessment—not the needs of the school, not the needs perceived by teachers, but the societal needs. When one has them, he can start applying system analysis and design techniques to the rest of the operation. When additional competency is needed, then the proper person should be called.

Question: How should a contract be handled in which one is trying to do something highly innovative?

Answer: Fixed fee plus incentive should be utilized. However it is necessary to be very specific about it. It is one thing to be innovative, but not to the extent of being etherial or mystic. When describing an innovation, there must be direction.

Question: A comment was made earlier about not obligating 100 percent of the funds. Please comment on that.

Answer: For technical assistance, one may want to hire a sub-contractor, an evaluator or an auditor; or he may want other kinds of management support. Perhaps the contractor can give the general system analysis and design, but not the "nitty-gritty" management on the technical service support—the logistic support. Money is needed for that. In other words, don't tie up all funds. There may be cost overruns. There may be time overruns. One can have all kinds of problems and should allow for the finances to meet these problems.

In summary, if the items mentioned in this chapter are taken into consideration, when initiating a performance contract, both the resultant educational program and the recipients of that program—the students—will benefit.

Albert V. Mayrhofer is administrative assistant to the associate commissioner of education, U.S. Office of Education.

EDUCATIONAL PROGRAM AUDIT

Robert E. Kraner

In the diversified educational system of the United States, one thing which has developed as a very essential part of every local educational system is the fiscal audit. It is difficult to think of a single school district that does not require a fiscal audit in becoming accountable for its use of fiscal funds. This same rationale for accountability of fiscal expenditures is now being expanded into another area of education, the instructional program. It would seem quite natural that, by taking this same concept of accountability and moving it into the area of student accomplishment, better relationships could be established between educational personnel and those interested in education: the administration, the teachers, the school boards, the parents, the community and, eventually, the students themselves.

As the writer uses and hears this new term—the

educational auditor—it reminds him somewhat of a good friend who was living as a missionary in Canada. He had a young boy three years old and, of course, was bringing him up in the correct manner. One morning the small child was coming in from play, and his mother admonished him, saying, "Now you be sure to wash your hands." "Why?" he asked. She replied, "Because you have germs on them." As he walked past his mother, shaking his head, he said, "Germs and Jesus—that's all I ever hear about, and I've never seen either one."

This may be the point where one is with the educational audit. A lot is heard about it, but as yet, nothing has been seen. It is the purpose of this chapter to "see" as much of the Educational Program Audit as possible.

EPIC is involved in five projects as the educational auditor, at the time of this writing. It is involved in the Texarkana Dropout Prevention Program, and in four bilingual programs within the state of Arizona. EPIC has implemented, changed directions, and modified. It has tried to uphold the audit guidelines from USOE. In following these guidelines, EPIC has tried to be a helpful force within the local project, and sincerely hopes that the first year of implementing this concept will prove beneficial to the U. S. Office of Education, to the state Departments of Education and, particularly, to the local project personnel.

Before considering the available USOE guidelines for the *educational audit* concept, the role of the auditor and a popular confusion experienced at the EPIC Evaluation Center should be mentioned. A basic misunderstanding that was encountered was that of failing to differentiate between the internal evaluation and the educational audit. More than ever, education, industry and government are participating cooperatively in local projects across the nation. In Titles VII and VIII, certain monies are required to be spent for the internal evaluation and for the educational audit. The internal evaluation is not the educational program audit.

The internal evaluation for a project may take place with people employed by the project and people working within the project, or it may be completed by an outside agency which is contracted to perform the functions of the internal evaluator. The internal evaluation, whether from inside or outside the project, produces results, interpretations and recommendations. The educational auditor, being familiar with the operation of the project, the objectives and the process activities of the project, will then verify the results derived by the internal evaluation.

In traveling and talking to people, it appeared that the function of the educational program audit was somewhat hazy. Many times, EPIC has been asked to audit a project. Actually, the correct question should have been, "Will you, as an outside source, come serve the function of the internal evaluator?" There has to be an internal evaluation before one is able to audit. There must be evaluation activity and results. If the functions of the internal evaluation are taking place, then the project is ready for the functions of the auditor.

"Independent Educational Accomplishment"

The general purpose of the educational audit is to verify the results of the project evaluation and to assess the appropriateness of the evaluation procedure. One must have results to verify, and one must have procedures to determine appropriateness. Each word of this title has a special significance to its meaning.

Independent. This refers to an outside, third party. EPIC practices this in many areas. If one is fortunate enough to have some money in the credit union, he can appreciate the audit that is made on the books of his credit union each year and the statement certifying that he does have the proper amount of money credited to his account and that his credit union is in fine standing. This comes from a third party, a disinterested outside source.

Educational. Regardless of one's feeling about this word, as it is used in most projects, it is mostly limited to what is called *basic skills.* The word "training" seems a bit limited, and the word "education" seems too global. When one considers education in this sense, he will think of the basic skills, knowledge and attitudes. The state of the art of measurement is such that one can measure quite effectively in these areas. There are a great many things that a project will be doing which will not be written down in terms of measurable behavioral objectives. Teachers, for example, are certainly free to go beyond the stated objectives. However, what is being audited, what is being measured and the concepts that are being held accountable are written down and are available for everyone to consider.

Accomplishment. This is the most important concept in accountability. This emphasis is upon learning rather than upon teaching. The accomplishment of the learner becomes the focus of the activity. This one emphasis alone will be enough to revolutionize education at all levels in the nation.

Audit. This is the standard review conducted by a trusted and qualified source. One of the most important considerations for the project director is the selection of an auditor. Is it someone he feels is competent? Is it someone who has the necessary expertise to make effective and meaningful recommendations for his project?

Considering all of the functions of the auditor, the need for a very diversified expertise can be seen. When one selects an auditor, he should try to select a person, or an agency, which can satisfy him in all these areas. The auditor is equally accountable for his performance.

The Contract

In talking with personnel from the U.S. Office of Education and with other interested people, it appears that they are most concerned that projects are not utilizing the available money to bring in needed expertise. Sometimes this money is being used for other things. Sometimes it is being turned back. The feedback received by EPIC is that project directors are being encouraged to utilize this money to bring about a better evaluation of their projects.

After an auditor has been selected, one of the next concerns is the contract. This contract should include the following elements:

1. Statement outlining the services and products which the auditor will provide in order to:
    a. verify the results of the project evaluation, and
    b. assess the appropriateness of the evaluation

procedures.

2. Names of audit personnel and a summary of their qualifications.

3. Specifications concerning the documents and services (such as secretarial, office space, transportation, and communication during the on-site visits) which The Local Education Agency (LEA) will provide the auditor.

4. Scheduling specifications, including approximate dates for submission of evaluation documents to auditor by LEA, approximate dates and minimum number and approximate length of audit visits, audit reporting dates, etc.

5. Specifications concerning the sampling techniques and procedures to be used by the auditor.

6. Specifications concerning the audit reports: their number, major topics to be included, who will prepare and certify them, to whom they will be submitted, approximate dates for submission, etc.

7. Specifications concerning the auditor's access to documents and persons, assurances of confidentiality, and any other special provisions required by the LEA or the auditor.

8. Contract budget and payment schedule.

9. Penalty and incentive.

The local projects are required to have a written contract with the audit agency under Titles VII and VIII. This contract usually relates payments to the delivery of certain products by the auditor.

As the auditor begins to work with a project, there are certain documents he will need. These are:

1.   Documents to be provided to the auditor prior to the beginning of the project.

     Federal Regulations.

     OE Guidelines and policy statements.

     Complete LEA proposal as approved—preliminary proposal, formal proposals and revisions.

     Pertinent correspondence between LEA and OE concerning proposal, such as evaluative comments and recommended revisions.

     Copies of specific evaluation instruments to be used.

     Copies of contract between LEA and evaluator, if evaluation is to be conducted externally.

2.   Documents to be retained by the LEA but available to the auditor for inspection at any time during the contract period:

     All data collected through project evaluation, including tests, questionnaires, interview sheets, rating sheets, observation schedules, material products, videotapes, films, etc.

     Project financial records.

3.   Documents to be submitted to the auditor by the

LEA at specified times prior to the auditor's on-site visits:

All tabulations, data analyses, and written summaries and interpretations of the results of project evaluation, including internal progress reports and quarterly reports submitted to OE.

Description of the data analysis techniques and procedures used by the project evaluator.

Evaluator's recommendations for revisions of the evaluation design and all recommendations for program modifications based on evaluation results.

Most of these documents are on file in the central office, the district office, or the business office of a school district. The educational auditor needs to read the original proposal, negotiation procedures and the modification to the actual proposal as they have emerged. He needs to be well aware of the inception and development of a project, in order to understand the full intent of the program.

As the project proceeds, the auditor conducts on-site visits and talks with the personnel. He examines results and makes reports to the project director. There are suggested report areas from the auditors. These are as follows:

1. Introductory and general comments concerning the quality of the project evaluation and the comparative findings of the project evaluation and the

audit.

2. Detailed critique of the product, process, and management evaluation conducted for each component, based on an assessment of the instruments used, data collection procedures, data analysis techniques and data analysis presentation.

3. Description of the auditor's on-site visit findings and their correlation with the evaluator's data and reports, on a component by component basis; summary of consistencies and discrepancies, and interpretation of the discrepancies.

4. Recommendations for revisions in the evaluation design, including a rationale for each recommendation. Since the auditor's objectivity can be retained only if the selection of a specific corrective action is a local decision, he should provide general rather than specific recommendations, posing several alternative actions or possible sources of assistance to the LEA in correcting the deficiency.

5. Confirmation or questioning of the need for program modifications which have been proposed as a result of project evaluation.

It should be stressed that the auditor makes his report to the project director—not to Washington, D.C. He does not make them to a magazine or to the local newspapers, although they somehow seem to get there. He makes the report back to the project director. The project director is the coordinating control of the audit, the internal evaluation and any performance contract of the local agency.

Generally, there will be three written reports from the audit agency to the project director, and these reports will reflect and project effectiveness in three areas. The three written reports include a Critique Report at the beginning of project operation, a Process Report approximately half way through the first year's operation and a Final Report which covers the entire year's operation.

Three areas of concern in these reports are *program management, instructional effectiveness,* and *cost effectiveness.* There seems to be very diverse opinions as to what these terms include. The EPIC Evaluation Center uses the terminology *management of project personnel, instructional effectiveness of the project,* and *instructional costs of the project,* hopefully, to limit the scope of concern of the audit until the diverse opinions are communicating.

Critique of Evaluation

U.S. Office of Education guidelines are available for the auditor's Critique of the Evaluation Design and procedures of the local project. These include the following:

A. Selection of Instruments
1. Did the range of instruments match the range of objectives?
2. Were the instruments valid—did they measure the actual behavior intended by the objectives?
3. Were the instruments reliable?
4. Were measures used for pretesting and post-testing suitable for such repetition?

B.   Data Collection Procedures
1.   Were the measures applied under the physical conditions required by the instruments?
2.   Were the testers, observers, or interviewers appropriately selected under the requirements of the instruments?
3.   Did the testers, observers, or interviewers receive appropriate training?
4.   Was the measurement schedule adhered to?

C.   Data Analysis Procedures
1.   Was there an adequate basis for any assumed equivalencies among groups?
2.   Were differential effects of the program treatment taken into consideration?
3.   Was the formula or source given for the statistical tests which were applied?
4.   Did the data meet the prerequisites for the statistical tests used?
5.   Was consideration given to important external factors which might have affected program results?

D.   Data Analysis Presentation
1.   Did the evaluator present the data in a clear form?
2.   Were statistical conclusions stated in language appropriate for the intended audience?
3.   Were the conclusions communicated prompt-

ly to the appropriate persons?

4.   Did the conclusions focus on areas of primary importance for program decision making?

Question: Should one insist upon a project using the EPIC Structure and Scheme for Evaluation when he serves as the auditor?

Answer: The selection of an evaluation design and the terminology to be used are not the prerogative of the auditor. This responsibility lies within the local project, or more specifically, with the internal evaluation. However, there are certain requirements, functions or strategies expected of any evaluation design which must be considered, regardless of terminology. Probably the most important outcome of the auditor's Critique Report is the establishment of a mutually satisfying framework of terminology and activity within which the evaluator and auditor can work cooperatively. In a fiscal audit, the agency and the bookkeeper agree early as to the system of bookkeeping, the information to be collected, critical points in time for sub-totals, etc. Although the educational audit is not synonymous with the fiscal audit, there is a commonality of need at the initial stage of operations for clear communication between evaluator and auditor.

Question: Just what are EPIC's requirements for an adequate evaluation program?

Answer: EPIC follows the USOE guidelines previously mentioned. However, using EPIC terminology, the requirements would be:

1) written behavioral objectives;
2) identification and description of variables;
3) evaluation design;
4) monitoring system; and
5) calendar of events.

Of course, these functions are examined in all four phases of the project operation: planning, implementing, product and recycling. When EPIC serves as the internal evaluator, this terminology is utilized. When EPIC serves as the auditor, a common communication system is developed and the terminology of the project is utilized.

Question: Can EPIC serve as both the internal evaluator and educational auditor?

Answer: No. This is impossible. Any agency can serve both functions in separate projects but cannot serve both functions in the same project. As a matter of fact, in 1971, EPIC will serve as the internal evaluator in two projects with which it served as the educational auditor in 1970. Another agency must serve as their auditor next year. As to the matter of switching roles, there would seem to be no difficulty going from the function of auditor to evaluator; however, going from the function of evaluator to auditor could destroy some of the desired objectivity of the audit.

Question: Shouldn't there be a concern that all of this evaluating, auditing, etc., will place too great an emphasis upon testing and measuring and that, in the long run, this influence will be detrimental to the student?

Answer: This concern brings to mind the story of the boy who graduated from college and returned home. His dad was very proud of him, and asked, "Son, what did you learn?" The boy thought, stammered, scratched his head, and said, "Well, I can't think of it, but if you give me four answers I can pick the right one." Certainly, this is not the type of behavior one desires in his students. By limiting the audit function to two percent of the total project, there is assurance that the tail will not wag the dog. The most essential part of every project is student learning. The audit should be considered as a small part of the total project operation, but, hopefully, a small part that will improve the project operation and those objectives that one is trying to achieve.

Question: What about some of these terms such as program management? If there is confusion as to their meaning, how can the audit possibly be performed?

Answer: Hopefully, guidelines and more specific definitions will be forthcoming. In the meantime, whatever is done in this area should reflect the best of the state of the art and should be presented in such a way as to provide useful information back to the project director to aid in his management processes. For example: EPIC looks very carefully at job descriptions and responsibilities. Many times management will have a specific task that needs to be performed. The project director asks, "Who is supposed to do this?" "A" says it is not in his contract. "B" says it is not in his contract. "C," etc. All of a sudden there are six people on contracts, and no one is really designated to do this specific task. In the calendar of events, EPIC requires that the date expected, the actual date, the person, the activity and the materials be planned for each project component or function and for the total project. These are a few simple procedures which aid immensely in the management of project personnel.

Question: What about the term, *cost effectiveness*? One hears a lot about cost but very little about effectiveness.

Answer: Unfortunately, the same is true at the EPIC center. However, as one reviews efforts made in cost effectiveness across the nation, he may become very optimistic about progress in this area. Rather than dwell on the negative, it seems more advantageous to consider what cost information can be retrieved and be helpful to the project or school district. Certainly, within a project direct instructional and personnel costs can be determined for the instructional program. These costs can be compared with the total project expenditure and broken down to a rate per pupil expenditure. The cost for adding to an instructional program can also be estimated. This falls short of the ideal, but such basic cost information can be very useful to a school district.

Question: It would seem that an audit report should be made public—to a board of directors, the community, etc. How does EPIC feel about this?

Answer: The auditor and the internal evaluator are still expected to report directly to the project director. Any outside source may then go to the project director for this information. A project director is chosen because of his knowledge and expertise in certain areas. Dealing with the public and disseminating information should be his responsibility.

Question: Will all of this talk about auditing really improve education, or is it just another fad?

Answer: This is a good question with which to conclude this report. Personally, the writer believes that public education, as it is known today, will not exist much longer in the United States unless the professionals in the education field take it upon themselves to become accountable to the public. I think the Educational Program Audit is the first of many specific activities that will develop into an integral part of the future American educational system.

Robert E. Kraner is an EPIC staff member, EPIC Evaluation Center, Tucson, Arizona.

Contents

This issue, at $3.00 per copy, is available, while the supply lasts, from Educational Technology Publications, 140 Sylvan Avenue, Englewood Cliffs, New Jersey 07632.